Paintings by ORI SHERMAN

The Four Questions

Text by Lynne Sharon Schwartz

LQ

LEVINE QUERIDO

Montclair • Amsterdam • New York

This is an Arthur A. Levine book
Published by Levine Querido

LEVINE QUERIDO

www.levinequerido.com · info@levinequerido.com

Levine Querido is distributed by Chronicle Books LLC

Ori Sherman's artwork was made available by The Magnes Collection of Jewish Art and Life,
U.C. Berkeley, who received the paintings as a gift from the artist.

Originally published in 1989 by Dial Books

Library of Congress Control Number: 2020935937
ISBN 978-1-64614-036-7

Printed and bound in China

Published in January 2021
Second Edition, First Printing

Book design by Atha Tehon and Semadar Megged
Calligraphy by Lili Cassel Wronker
The text type set in ITC Galliard Std

The art for this book was created using gouache, a painting technique in which opaque colors are
ground in water and mixed with a preparation of gum. Each painting was then color-separated and
reproduced in full color.

The photography of the artwork for this edition was done by Sibila Savage Photography.

To my parents, Earl and Anna Sherman, may they rest in peace,

who made my first seders such beautiful and memorable experiences;

and to my friends Charles Little, Dominic Martello, and Richard Schwarzenberger,

who have enriched my life; and to all my brothers and sisters, both human and animal,

who are not yet free, I dedicate this book.

O.S.

For my nieces, Dara and Jaclyn Sharon

L.S.S.

On a certain night each year when the dark of winter is passing and the world is warming up for the green of spring, Jews in all lands gather to celebrate a joyful holiday. Passover, or Pesach. The house is sparkling clean and everyone is dressed up and the table is set with new dishes and glasses. Everybody has a glass of wine to drink and a book, the Haggadah, with the Passover story and songs.

On the Seder plate in the center of the table are special foods, foods not eaten on ordinary nights. At Seder tables around the world the children ask, What are we celebrating? Why these special foods?

Why is this night different from all other nights?

מַה נִּשְׁתַּנָּה הַלַּיְלָה הַזֶּה מִכָּל הַלֵּילוֹת ؟

The mothers and fathers answer: Long ago we were slaves in the land of Egypt. And after years of hard work and bitter sorrow, God led us out of Egypt and set us free. We celebrate to give thanks and to remember how we won our freedom. We do more than remember, though. We tell how it happened and eat the foods and drink the wine so we can feel the story happening to us as it did to the Jews long ago.

Each one of us is free because of what happened in Egypt, and so the Passover Seder is a feast of welcome, of family and friends coming together in gratitude. The door is open. Let all who are hungry come and eat. Let all who are lonely come and join the family. Let all who are curious come and see how we celebrate. And let the prophet Elijah enter and drink a cup of wine too.

The shankbone on the Seder plate reminds us of the lambs the ancient Jews used to offer to God at their spring holiday in hopes of a good harvest.

The roasted egg on the plate means the birth of a new season and a new life. For just as fresh young creatures break out of an egg, the Jews came to life as a nation when God freed them with his strong hand and outstretched arm.

It happened this way.

God chose Moses to go to Pharaoh, the leader of the Egyptians, and say: "It is wrong to keep anyone in slavery. Let my people go."

But Pharaoh refused.

God sent down plagues to frighten the Egyptians so Pharaoh would obey. First he turned the rivers to blood so the fish died and the water was spoiled—no one could drink. He sent thousands of frogs to creep through the land, and then lice to itch, and swarming gnats to torment the people. He sent a sickness that killed all the cattle. He made boils break out on everyone's skin. Hail and lightning destroyed the trees and crops, and locusts ruined whatever growing things were left. And as if that were not enough, God sent a thick darkness that covered the land for three days.

With each plague, Pharaoh promised to free the Jews. But when the plague was over, he went back on his word and said no.

Finally God sent a tenth plague, the worst of all. He sent down the Angel of Death to kill the firstborn son of every Egyptian family.

It was the night of the Jews' spring holiday, when every family sacrificed a lamb to God. Moses told the Jews: "Dip a leafy branch in the lambs' blood and sprinkle a few drops on your doorposts. That way the Angel of Death will recognize you and pass over your houses and not kill your children."

And the Jews did, and the Angel of Death passed over their houses. So our holiday of remembrance is called Passover.

Meanwhile Pharaoh was wakened in the middle of the night by a great cry. When he saw what had happened, when he heard the Egyptians in every house shouting and weeping for their children, he told the Jews: "Go. Your God is too strong for me. Leave Egypt this very night, and be gone by morning."

The Jews packed their things in a tremendous hurry and sped from Egypt, following Moses into the wilderness. God showed the way, leading them with a pillar of cloud by day and a pillar of fire by night.

But back in Egypt, Pharaoh changed his mind again. He sent his army to bring the Jews back and make them slaves once more. The Jews had just reached the shores of the Red Sea when the Egyptian army overtook them. They could not bear to return to slavery. But how could they escape with the sea before them? There seemed no way out.

God told Moses to raise his hand, and as he did, a miraculous thing happened. The waters parted and the Jews passed safely through a path of dry ground in the Red Sea, with high walls of water glistening on either side. When the Egyptian soldiers tried to follow on their horses, the glistening walls of water tumbled over them and they sank to the bottom and drowned.

At last the Jews were safe. In the years they spent in the desert with Moses they learned how to be a community, living with just laws and treasuring freedom.

• • •

But, the children still ask, What about the other foods on the Seder plate?

On all other nights we eat either bread or matzoh.
Why tonight do we eat only matzoh?

שֶׁבְּכָל הַלֵּילוֹת אָנוּ אוֹכְלִין חָמֵץ וּמַצָּה
הַלַּיְלָה הַזֶּה כֻּלּוֹ מַצָּה:

When Pharaoh ordered the Jews to be gone by morning, they were in such a rush that they couldn't even wait for the dough in the ovens to rise and become bread. They just grabbed the dough and fled.

At the Seder we eat *matzoh*, which is unleavened bread, to taste what our ancestors ate on their flight. Even though it is flat and hard and called "the bread of affliction," or sorrow, we eat it with joy. It is the bread of freedom too.

On all other nights we eat all kinds of herbs.
Why tonight do we eat only bitter herbs?

שֶׁבְּכָל הַלֵּילוֹת אָנוּ אוֹכְלִין שְׁאָר יְרָקוֹת, הַלַּיְלָה הַזֶּה מָרוֹר:

We eat the bitter herbs because it was so bitter being slaves. The work was long and hard and the masters were cruel. But most bitter of all, we were not our own people—we could not live and work as we pleased. Now our freedom feels more precious as we remember and taste the bitterness where it began.

We eat the bitter herbs along with the *haroses* on the Seder plate—the nuts and apples and wine mixed together. Haroses tastes sweet, like the sweetness of hope, but it looks like the mortar the Jews in Egypt used to make bricks. For that was the work our slave ancestors did, making bricks all day in the hot sun, to build the pyramids and storehouses of the Egyptian cities of Pithom and Raamses.

On all other nights we eat herbs without
dipping them into anything.
Why tonight do we dip them twice into salt water?

הַלַּיְלָה הַזֶּה שְׁתֵּי פְעָמִים:
שֶׁבְּכָל הַלֵּילוֹת אֵין אָנוּ מַטְבִּילִין אֲפִילוּ פַּעַם אֶחָת

First we dip the greens, which remind us of spring and hope, into salt water to taste the salty tears the slaves shed. For imagine how they must have wept, hating their slavery and wishing for a way to be free.

We dip the herbs a second time to remember the Angel of Death passing over our houses. For, obeying what Moses told them, the Jews in Egypt dipped a leafy branch into the sacrificed lambs' blood and sprinkled it on their doors to keep their children safe from the Angel of Death.

Because Pharaoh was stubborn and refused to free the Jews, many of the Egyptians died of the plagues as well as in the Red Sea. When we drink the wine at the Seder table, we spill some drops to show that our joy is not complete and pure. How can it be, God asks, when so many of his children in both nations died in the struggle for freedom?

On all other nights we eat either sitting up or reclining.
Why tonight do we all recline?

ٮڲۭڲٮ ٮٮٮ ڇڲٮ ٮٱٮٮٮ:
ٱٮٮڲ ٮڲۭڲٮٮ ٸٮٮ ٸٮڲۭٮ ٮٮ ٮٱٮٮ ٮٮٮ ٮٱٮٮٮ

When we were slaves in Egypt we worked all day, through years of pain and weariness, with never a moment to rest. We could not do as free people do, which is to work their share and then rest and enjoy themselves as they please. Now we can feast together as free men and women and children, and lean back and eat the good things at the Seder. We recline to show we are no longer slaves. We have no masters, and never will again.

At the Passover Seder we remember that terrible and then wonderful time, and in the remembering, the terror and the wonder happen to us. We were once slaves, now we enjoy freedom. Together we wish that by next year's Seder, all people living in slavery, any place in the world, will pass over to freedom.

———————————————————— ✡ ————————————————————

The Order of the Passover Seder

1 · Kadesh: Blessings before the meal.

2 · U'rechatz: Washing of the hands.

3 · Karpas: Eating and dipping of a green vegetable.

4 · Yachatz: Breaking the middle matzoh.

5 · Magid: Asking the four questions and telling the Passover story.

6 · Rachatz: Washing the hands again.

7 · Motzi matzoh: Eating the matzoh.

8 · Maror Korech: Eating the bitter herbs with matzoh.

9 · Shulchan Orech: Serving the traditional meal.

10 · Tzafun: Finding the Afikomen and eating it.

11 · Barech: Saying the blessings after the meal.

12 · Hallel nirtzah: Concluding the service with songs of praise and
thanks to God.

FROM SUMER TO ORI SHERMAN

Throughout history, humans have thought about—and depicted—all kinds of forms beyond those they saw in nature. We have dreamed up unnatural and supernatural beings by combining elements that do occur naturally. A common example of this is when we have imposed human features on non-humans—on rocks, trees, flowers, and of course, animals. Art history offers a diversely-colored tapestry of such images, from the serious to the silly—from ancient religious imagery to Babar and modern Mickey Mouse cartoons.

The ancient Egyptians offer an early example of the "serious" sort, with hieroglyphic images shaped between five and three thousand years ago that depict many of their gods with human bodies and animal heads—scarab beetles, jackals, lions, crocodiles, and falcon-hawks, to name a few. They believed that their divinities possessed the qualities of these animals in supernatural abundance.

That sort of imagery would re-emerge in the Jewish tradition thousands of years later in illuminated manuscripts from the Ashkenazi world—the oldest and most famous of which is the so-called *Birds' Head Haggadah* (ca 1300). Interestingly, the *Birds' Head Haggadah* may be the flip-side of those Egyptian hieroglyphs: Here, they depict bird-headed celebrants not to represent gods, but to avoid offending the One God by presuming to shape human figures themselves. (That being something only God does.) Or perhaps the anonymous *Birds' Head* artist was consciously referencing Egyptian gods; instead of making the otherwise downtrodden Jews into creatures seen by their neighbors as somewhere between human and animal, the artist rather made them into creatures between human and divine, as they prepared for and celebrated the Passover Seder.

In any case, while the Egyptians were imaging their gods, the Sumerians in Mesopotamia were depicting diverse creatures—foxes, scorpions, lions, sheep, and others—simply with human attributes. They devised such anthropomorphized animals most famously on the four gold leaf- and lapis lazuli-decorated harps found in tombs dating from more than four millennia ago. On these harps, animals stand up on their hind legs and carry ewers of water, or play harps themselves. These simultaneously serious and light-hearted images grew from tales later known as the Greek fables associated with Aesop, which would eventually be passed down to our own time through the Romans and subsequent literary tradition.

The artistic mode of humanizing animals continued in the Jewish visual world, for example, in the interior décor of the timber synagogues of Eastern Europe. The curved inner carapace of the roof of the 1642 (some say 1652) Chodorow synagogue and the ceiling and walls of the early 18th-century synagogue of Mogilev, for instance, were overrun not only with animals, but with animals that seemed virtually human in their stances, activities, and expressions.

Chodorow's ceiling was painted by the itinerant Jewish artist Israel Ben Mordecai Lissnicki, who added animals, like monkeys and unicorns, that the Sumerians never imagined. In one image an upright lion trumpets on the horn of an upright unicorn, a symbol of the hoped-for Messianic era. The Mogilev synagogue images would inspire one of the most important Jewish artists in early twentieth-century Tsarist (and post-Tsarist) Russia, El Lissitzky, who, visiting as a 22-year-old, asked rhetorically: "…is that face of a lion in the drawings of the zodiac in the synagogue of Moghilev not the face of a rabbi?"

It is this broad tapestry of anthropomorphized animals into which Ori Sherman weaves his lush, brilliantly-hued threads in illustrating *The Four Questions*. Sherman's vibrant forms synthesize a unique Eastern European Jewish visual heritage with an ancestry in Sumer and influences extending from Arabo-Islamic decor to Shalom of Safed to *Stuart Little*, offering a visual tour-de-force that is a perfect complement to the splendid text of Lynne Sharon Schwartz.

Ori Z. Soltes
Georgetown University
Author, *Tradition and Transformation: A Comprehensive Exploration of Three Millennia of Jewish Art & Architecture*